SEA SPONGES

A Buddy Book by
Deborah Coldiron

ABDO
Publishing Company

UNDERWATER WORLD

VISIT US AT

www.abdopublishing.com

Published by ABDO Publishing Company, 8000 West 78th Street, Edina, Minnesota 55439.

Printed in the United States.

Coordinating Series Editor: Sarah Tieck
Contributing Editor: Michael P. Goecke
Graphic Design: Deborah Coldiron
Cover Photograph: Photos.com
Interior Photographs/Illustrations: Clipart.com (page 11); Brandon Cole Marine Photography (pages 15, 17, 19, 25); Minden Pictures: Sue Daly/npl (page 21), Jurgen Freund/npl (page 21), Kim Taylor/npl (pages 20, 21, 28), D.P. Wilson/FLPA (page 23); Photos.com (pages 5, 7, 13, 27, 29, 30); Jeff Rotman Photography (page 9)

Library of Congress Cataloging-in-Publication Data

Coldiron, Deborah.
    Sea sponges / Deborah Coldiron.
        p. cm.—(Underwater World)
    Includes index.
    ISBN 978-1-59928-812-3
    1. Sponges—Juvenile literature. I. Title.

QL371.6.C65 2007
593.4—dc22

                                                    2007017851

Table Of Contents

The World Of Sea Sponges

Every living creature needs water. Some animals not only need water, they live in it, too.

Scientists have found more than 250,000 kinds of plants and animals living underwater. And, they believe there could be one million more! The sea sponge is one animal that lives in this underwater world.

Seventy percent of Earth's surface is covered in water. Sea sponges make this underwater world their home.

Sea sponges come in a wide variety of colors, shapes, and sizes. These unusual animals live in both shallow and deep waters. They attach themselves to rocks, plants, and other surfaces.

FAST FACTS

Scientists once said sea sponges were plants. Today, they know sponges are animals.

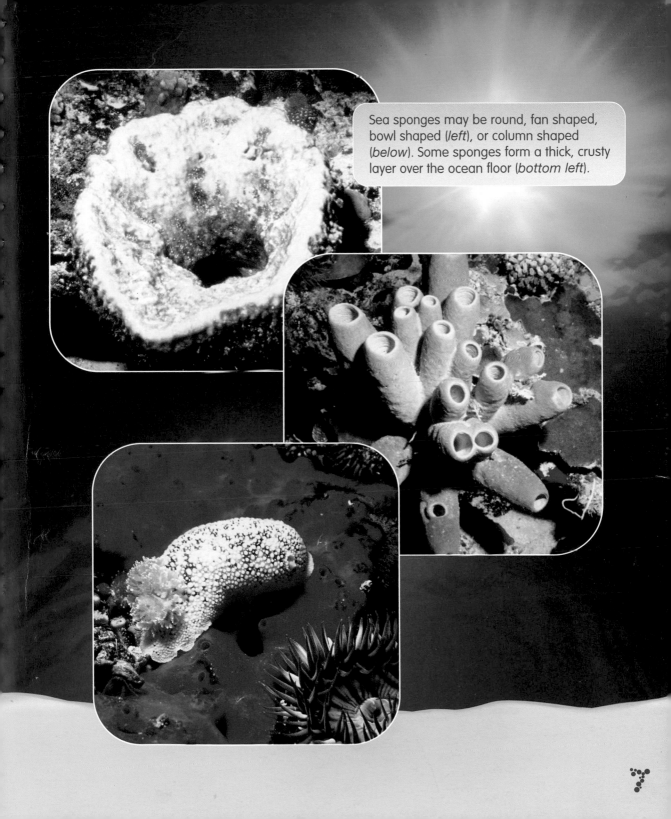

Sea sponges may be round, fan shaped, bowl shaped (*left*), or column shaped (*below*). Some sponges form a thick, crusty layer over the ocean floor (*bottom left*).

There are about 5,000 **species** of sea sponges in our underwater world. Most of them live at the bottom of the ocean. Around 150 sponge species are found in freshwater lakes and rivers.

The smallest sea sponges are shorter than one inch (3 cm). But, some sponges grow to four feet (1 m)!

Barrel sponges are among the world's largest sponges.

A Closer Look

Sea sponges have simple bodies. They don't have heads, eyes, brains, arms, legs, or ears. They don't have muscles, **nerves**, or **internal** organs either.

Sea sponge bodies are **filters**. To survive, sponges move **nutrient**-rich water throughout their bodies.

The Body Of A Sea Sponge

Osculum

Ostia

To do this, sponges use two types of body openings. They have small **pores** called ostia that take in water. And, they have a single, larger opening called the osculum. This pushes out water and waste.

Sea sponges have skeletons. These are usually made of tiny toothpick shaped **minerals**, such as limestone or silica. These are called spicules.

Other sea sponges have skeletons made of bits of **protein** called spongins. And, a few sponges have skeletons made of both spicules and spongins.

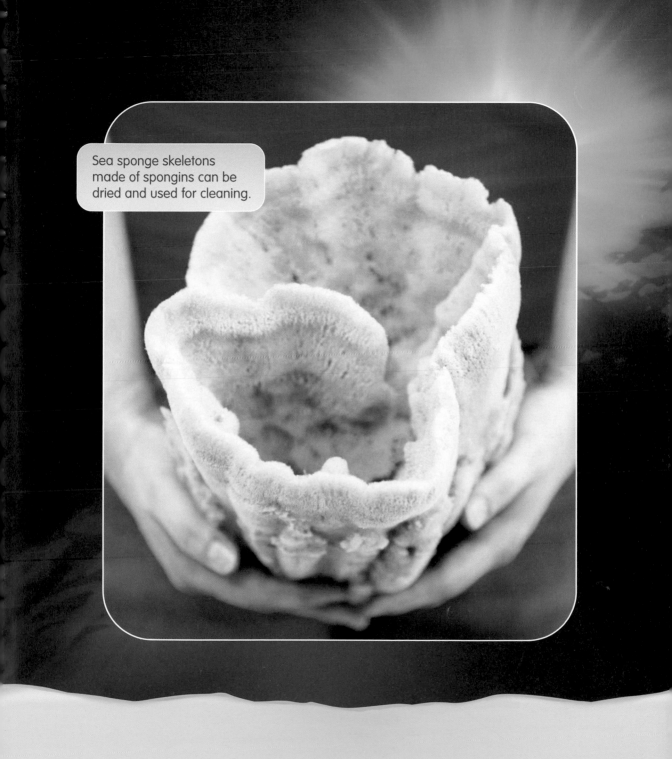

Sea sponge skeletons made of spongins can be dried and used for cleaning.

The sea sponge's skeleton has important jobs. It provides important support for the body. It helps hold the sponge together, even in rough waters.

The skeleton also protects the sponge. It discourages predators from eating the sponge or invading its body.

FAST FACTS

For hundreds of years, people have used sea sponges for tasks such as bathing, painting, and cleaning.

Giant Orange
Elephant Ear Sponge

A Growing Sea Sponge

Sea sponges reproduce in more than one way. One way is called budding. When this happens, small buds grow on the sponge's body. A new sponge can form when a bud breaks off.

One of many sponge buds

Some sponges produce many buds.

Other sea sponges begin life as eggs inside a parent's body. The eggs are **fertilized** by other sponges.

The fertilized eggs develop into larvae. Then the parent sponges release the larvae, which swim away.

Finally, the larvae settle on the ocean floor. There, they attach to surfaces such as rock. From each larva, a new sponge begins to grow.

FAST FACTS

Most sponges are hermaphrodites. That means a sponge may act as either male or female when reproducing.

Young boring sponges look for coral to grow on. These sponges can do a lot of damage to a coral reef.

Family Fun

Sea sponges are very simple animals. Scientists say sponges have lived in Earth's waters for about 500 million years!

Sea sponges form a group of animals called porifera. There are no other animals within this group.

Scientists divide sponge **species** into three different groups. The groups are chosen based on the makeup of a sponge's skeleton.

Glass sponges have skeletons made of silica. The spicules within a glass sponge's skeleton form very complex patterns. Many people find them quite beautiful.

About 90 percent of sponges are demosponges. These are the sponges people use for bathing, painting, and cleaning. Their skeletons are made of soft spicules called spongins. They often have silica spicules as well.

Red boring sponges (*above*) and hedgehog sponges (*left*) are demosponges.

Calcareous sponges have skeletons made of limestone. Most of these sponges live in shallow waters. However, some have been found in the deep sea.

A Quiet Neighborhood

Sea sponges are found in many areas of our oceans. So, they have many neighbors.

One of the sea sponge's most common neighbors is plankton. Sea sponges feed on these tiny plants and animals as they quietly drift along the ocean surface. Many other ocean animals, such as the whale shark, also eat plankton.

Plankton is made up of tiny plants and
animals that drift in the ocean.
Scientists call the animals zooplankton.
The plants are known as phytoplankton.

Inhaling Dinner

Sea sponges do not have mouths, stomachs, or intestines. Instead, they rely on their water-**filtering** abilities to take in food.

Sea sponges draw in water through their **pores**. The sponge captures plankton from the water. Then, it pushes out water and waste back into the ocean.

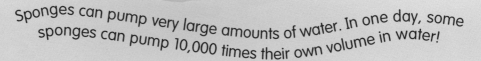

FAST FACTS Sponges can pump very large amounts of water. In one day, some sponges can pump 10,000 times their own volume in water!

Some animals, such as crinoids, take shelter in sea sponges. These plankton-feeding creatures eat some of the food drawn in by the sponge.

A Sensitive Species

The oceans are unsafe for sea sponges. They are sensitive to changes in their **environments**. And, they can easily catch diseases.

Sponges have few predators, however. Many sponges produce **toxins** that discourage animals from eating them.

FAST FACTS

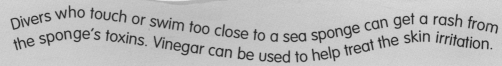

Divers who touch or swim too close to a sea sponge can get a rash from the sponge's toxins. Vinegar can be used to help treat the skin irritation.

Some fish, such as gray angelfish, are not harmed by sea sponge toxins. These fish feed on sea sponges.

Fascinating Facts

Venus Flower Basket
Sponge Skeleton

🌿 In Japan, the Venus flower basket sponge is considered a symbol of eternal love.

🌿 Sea sponges can regenerate. If a sponge breaks apart, the surviving cells can combine to form a new sponge.

🪸 Loofah sponges are often used for bathing. Many people think they are dried sea sponges. But, loofahs actually come from the fruit of a tropical plant.

Loofah Sponges

Learn And Explore

Sea sponges may hold the answers to many medical questions. Some scientists are studying the chemicals found in sponges. They are hoping to create new medications from them.

In fact, one of the first **cancer**-treating drugs was made from a sea sponge chemical.

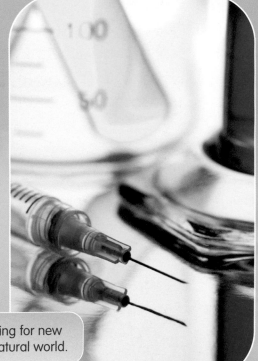

Scientists are constantly looking for new sources of medicine in our natural world.

IMPORTANT WORDS

cancer   a disease that attacks the body.

environment   all the surroundings that affect the growth and well-being of a living thing.

fertilize   able to produce seeds, fruit, or young.

filter   a material with tiny openings through which liquid passes. When liquid passes through the filter, it catches objects and separates them.

internal   inside.

mineral   a natural substance. Minerals make up other parts of nature, such as rocks.

nerve   a part of the body that produces physical feelings.

nutrient   a substance found in food and used in the body to promote growth, maintenance, and repair.

pore   a small opening in an animal or plant through which matter passes.

protein   an important nutrient in the diet of all animals.

species   living things that are very much alike.

toxin   a substance that is harmful.

WEB SITES

To learn more about sea sponges, visit ABDO Publishing Company on the World Wide Web. Web sites about sea sponges are featured on our Book Links page. These links are routinely monitored and updated to provide the most current information available.

www.abdopublishing.com

INDEX